AF379513

FROM THE INSIDE OUT

Who Are You?

DR. RENECIA WILLIAMS

Wasteland Press
www.wastelandpress.net
Shelbyville, KY USA

From The Inside Out:
Who are You?
by Dr. Renecia Williams

First Printing – August 2015
ISBN: 978-1-68111-057-8
Back cover photo by Derrick Trice of Dean Trice Photography
Copyright © 2015 Derrick Trice. All Rights Reserved.

Unless otherwise noted, all scriptures quotations are
From the King James Version of the Bible.

Scriptures quotations marked AMP are from the Amplified Bible.
Scriptures quotations marked Message are from the Message bible.
Scriptures marked ESV are from the English Standard Version bible.
Webster Dictionary

Printed in the U.S.A.

0   1   2   3   4   5

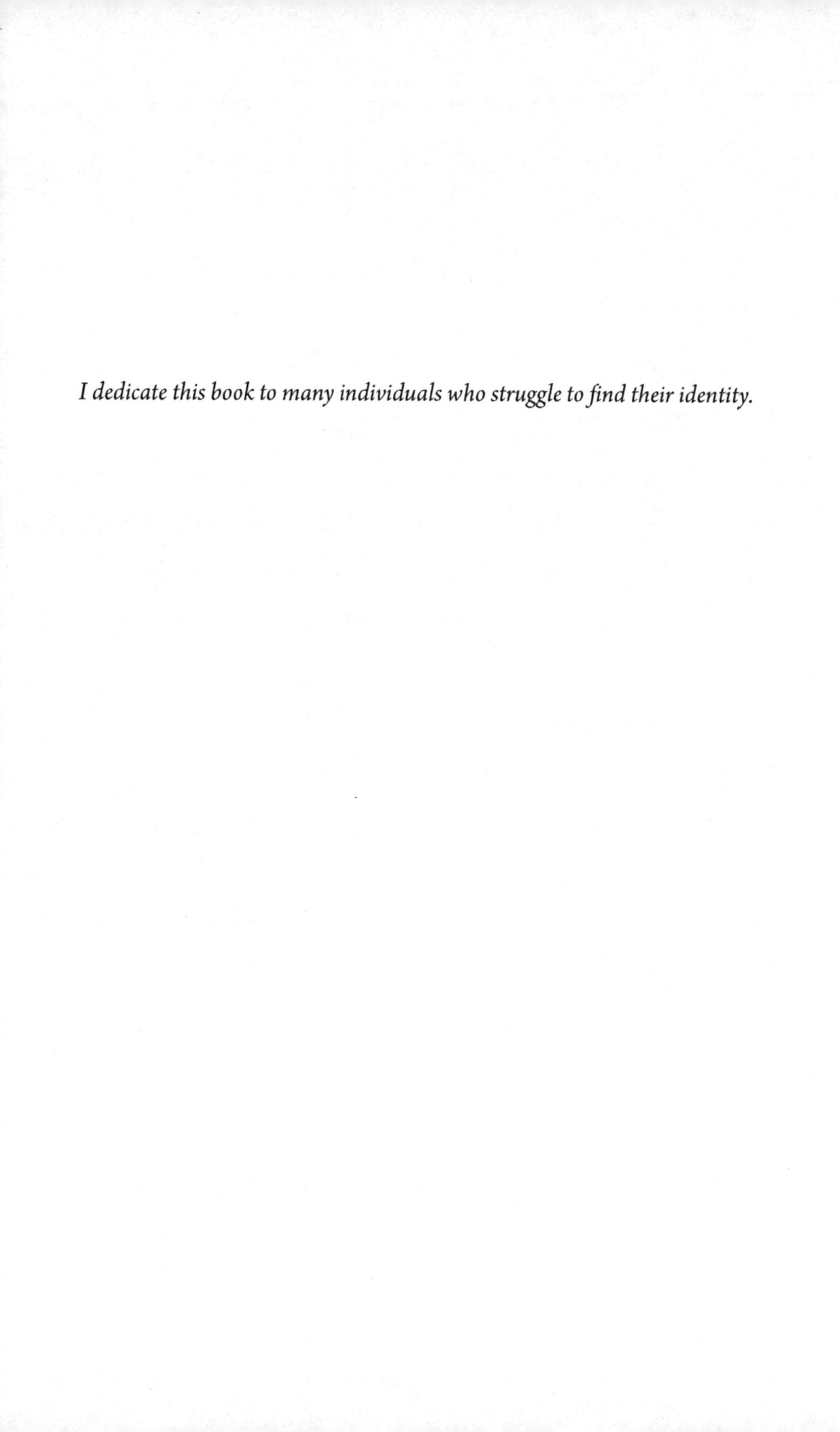

I dedicate this book to many individuals who struggle to find their identity.

ACKNOWLEDGEMENTS

First and foremost, I would like to thank God who has given me the grace to complete such an assignment while trouble was all around me. Only He gave me the strength to move forward.

I want to thank my children, Parker and Autumn, who gave me kisses and hugs whenever I thought I was going to fall apart. I love you both always. Always remember that nothing is impossible when God and His word are the final authority in your lives.

To my mother, Phyllis Moore, who has stood in the gap for me when I felt as though I had no legs to stand on. Thank you for your continued support. Even when I did not make the right choices, you always got me back on track. I love you.

To my father, Willie Moore III, thanks so much for believing in me and in the vision that God has given me. No matter how many delays we encountered, you were always there to help move things along smoothly. I want you to know that I truly appreciate you and love you dearly.

To my niece, Kayla Plummer, you were part of the inspiration that I needed to complete this book. It was your determination to find purpose and your many questions about life that gave me the extra push that I needed to finish this book. Allow it to be your inspiration to do exactly what God has called you to do. You are a very special and unique young lady; never settle for anything that is not God's best. I love you. Never give up!

To those of you who have prayed for me, even when I did not realize I needed prayer, I thank God for you. May God continue to bless you for your obedience in assisting me with sending this word of truth throughout the world.

Last but not least, to my best friend, number one fan, and soul mate, you have been here for me during the birthing process of this book. As my birthing instructor, you taught me to push, no matter how much pain I felt. You also supported me financially and in prayer. I want you to know that I love and appreciate you. The best is yet to come.

CONTENTS

1

From The Inside Out

Millions of people all over the world have no clue about how they were originally created and the purpose of their creation. We are not people who happened to have landed on a place called Earth. There is a root to every fruit; nothing just happens. God did not create a chair and table with clear purpose and identity, only to create His children to wonder who they are and what their purpose is. No, it is actually the opposite. He created us with purpose and identity, but the problem has been that many have not been taught who they are and how they should live. Most are trying to live from the outside in, instead of living from the inside out.

I encourage you to read this book as many times as it takes for revelation to flow freely. It is vital that we know who we are in order for the world not to have any say-so about our true identity. God loves us so much, and it is His plan that not any shall perish.

2

Whom Am I?

I remember when I was a little girl, there was a long mirror on the outside of the bathroom door. I would stand in front of that mirror, look at myself, and say, "Who are you?" I would look at my skin and open up my eyes really wide to try and see if I could see anything different about myself. I knew there had to be way more to me than what I could see and naturally feel.

After carefully evaluating the skin on my face and neck and not seeing anything that appeared to be different about who I am, I decided one day to open up my mouth to see if I could look down my throat and see if I could find any answers in there. Again, I found nothing special. So one day, I decided to open up my mouth and sing. I then asked my mom, "Where does the sound come from that comes out of our mouths?" While I was growing up, my mom was the type of person that if she did not know the answer, she would just simply say, "Girl, be quiet."

At the tender age of five, my mind was racing. No adult that I asked could tell me what was inside of me, outside of answers that a doctor would offer. I knew in my heart, even as I approached my teenage years and into early adulthood, that there had to be more to me than what I could see, touch or smell. It wasn't until I met my pastor in 1999 that I discovered the answers to all of my questions.

Genesis 1:26 Let us make man in our image. We know that God is trinity; therefore HE has created His children as a trinity as well. God is Father, Son, and Holy Spirit. Man is created as body, soul, and spirit. Our body is the house in which we really reside. ***Therefore, we are a spirit that lives in a body that has a soul.***

Genesis 2:7 Then the Lord God formed the man of dust from the ground and breathed into his nostrils the breath of life, and the man became a living creature. In order for there to be nostrils, the body had to have been here on Earth first. However, notice there was no life even though there was a body. God had to take His breath and place it inside of us before we could become a living creature. This can only mean that ***we live from the inside out.***

Often we pay so much attention to our flesh, not realizing that the flesh is nothing without us being in it. Our skin color is merely the design that God created for us to dwell in while on Earth. It is primarily the same way an architect designs a house. All houses are different sizes and colors. Some are made with aluminum siding while others are constructed of brick. When a person drives past a friend's house, it is natural for them to say, "That's my friend's house." That is totally correct. The house belongs to the friend, and the friend resides in the house.

Our body is the house in which we live in. When our spirit leaves our body on Earth and relocates to heaven or hell, the house will be left empty here on Earth, and because we are no longer in it to keep it in full operation, it will eventually go back to the dust. In order to get a better understanding of how we operate, we must know the differences between our soul, spirit, and body.

3

Soul, Spirit, and Body

Before we find out how we operate, let's first take a look at how God operates. He is God the Father, Son, and Holy Spirit. The Father has many names, and He is able to operate on many different levels. He is not just subjected or limited to one operation, for He is many. I like to look at the trinity as a corporation. We have the CEO, which is the Father. We have the son who sits at the right of the Father and operates as the director; and we then have the Holy Spirit who is the field supervisor. In a corporation, you have to go through the chain of command before you can get to the CEO. Therefore, you must go through Jesus to get to the Father. "Jesus saith unto him, I am the way, the truth, and the life: no man cometh unto the Father, but by me." *John 14:6*. The Holy Spirit is the field supervisor, and He is available here on Earth to aid and assist us along the way. When we are not able to understand what the supervisor's instructions are, we can then put in a petition or request to the CEO by using Jesus' name to get the help that we need. This is also known as prayer. It is important to understand all roles in order to get the results that are desired. This is also true as we deal with the soul, body, and spirit.

The soul is where our mind, will, imagination, intellect, and emotions reside. This is the area where our earthly experiences or our humanistic characteristics are located. The Hebrew word for soul is *nephesh*, which means the feelings, passions, desires, and appetites of any living thing. Our soul plays an important part of who we are and what we become.

The ***mind*** is a very powerful tool that lies hidden inside of us but can be seen based on how an individual functions. ***The mind consists of two interconnecting parts, which are called the conscious and the subconscious.*** The conscious part of the mind functions through the body's brain, which allows us to move around in the physical part of us known as the body. The conscious also operates and deals with the reality of things. The subconscious is the storehouse also known as the memory. The best way to understand the subconscious mind is by understanding the phrase "I will forgive you but I will never forget." When something happens to a person that changes their direction in life, it is stored in the subconscious. This does not mean that the individual is thinking of the incident daily, but if it is brought back up, the subconscious mind will send a download of the event, and that may cause our feelings and emotions to get involved.

Our thoughts are shaped by the ingredients that have been placed in the mind. This is why the bible states *"Finally, brethren, whatsoever things are true, whatsoever things are honest, whatsoever things are just, whatsoever things are pure, whatsoever things are lovely, whatsoever things are of good report; if there be any virtue, and if there be any praise, think on these things." Philippians 4:8* It is important that we place ourselves in environments that are conducive to our personal growth. Our mind can be governed either by negativity or positivity. Where we end up in life has a lot to do with how we think or perceive ourselves.

Our will is directly connected to our thought life. Our determination to succeed in life is grounded by our thoughts. Have you ever heard a person say that they are strong-willed? Well, most of the time that person is that way because of how they think. They are determined to be better than what they were yesterday because they know they can be. We must stay focused on the promises of God and keep our mind stayed on Him in order to strengthen our will and most importantly have it line up with the purpose and plan of God for our lives. God has designed us to have a free will. *Deuteronomy 30:19 "I call heaven and earth to record this day against you, that I have set before you life and death, blessing and cursing: therefore choose life that both thou and thy seed may live."* He was so kind in the scripture to give us the answer to choose life.

Our ***imagination*** is dominated by the senses and also by what we think. We can daydream and imagine being somewhere based on what we have seen, heard or experienced. Have you ever heard, "The sky is the limit"? One of the reasons that people feel that the sky is the limit is because that is how far they can see in the natural, and, in most cases, they cannot think past what they can see in the natural. The bible states, *"as a man thinks so is he." Proverbs 23:7* Some cannot see themselves going any further than where someone else has gone. You will discover later in this book that you can go as far as you want to go and where no one has been when you have the right information and tools.

The ***intellect*** deals with knowledge and experience. In most cases, this is what most people depend on to make decisions in life. It has been stated that the intellect and ***emotions*** work together. The way we think essentially will tell us how to feel, and our feelings are directly tied to our emotions. If a person is in fear, they are in fear because of something that they know or have experienced; therefore, the intellect has programmed this fear and sends a signal to the emotions, so we can start to act the way that we are thinking or feeling.

Emotions express our feelings. What we are thinking will eventually show in what we are expressing on the outside. If a person is thinking sad thoughts, it may promote tears. This is also true if a person's mindset is in a happy place; we may see smiles and even hear the sounds of laughter. Emotions can ultimately take over and rule our mind and body. A person will start to say things like, "I don't feel like going to work or I don't feel like you love me anymore, etc." All of these feelings become like a virus in the inside of us and begin to spread in our physical appearance, and then we begin to start looking like our inner feelings.

Have you ever decided that you needed to work out for some reason or another? You had not been in the gym for years, and you decided to return. Well, some days you are not going to feel like going to the gym. However, you can start to program your thoughts by saying "I can do this" and start remembering the reason that you decided to work out in the first place and get your emotions and feelings in line with what is most important, and then head out to the gym and have the best workout ever. It is very important that we do not allow what we feel at any given time to dominate what is most important. ***Feelings are like facts and facts are subject to change.*** It may be a fact that you don't feel like doing something at a certain time, but you can do something to change that feeling. However, the truth remains the same. It is true that we all need to exercise. No matter how small or large we are, exercise is vital to live a long and healthy life.

Our ***body*** is the temple/house where we are temporarily located until our time on Earth is complete. Our body is like a legal suit. God saw fit that since we are spirits and spirits cannot be seen, we needed to have something covering us so that others can identify who we are while on Earth. Jesus who walked the Earth had to have a body in which he lived while completing his assignment here. Everyone comes to Earth in a legal suit that we call the body. The body represents the physical and tangible part of us. However, as mentioned earlier, the inside of us dictates how the physical part of us functions.

So far, we have covered all of the natural parts to mankind. The soul, mind, and our physical existence called the body. However, there still remains a very important part of us called the spirit.

4

The Spirit

All things reproduce after its own kind. Two horses will produce ponies, which will eventually become horses. Nothing or no one can create anything without implementing its own DNA inside of it. *John 4:24 states that God is a spirit. Genesis 1:27 states, "So God created mankind in his own image. In the image of God he created him; male and female he created them."*

We are spiritual beings having a natural experience on Earth. God is a spirit being, not the sun, moon or stars. He is not the air, wind or universal mind. He is not black, white, Hispanic, etc. **God is a person with a spirit.** His body is of a spirit substance instead of flesh and bones. God is currently not on the earth in the flesh; therefore, He does not have to have an earth suit or to look like us in the flesh.

In *Daniel 10 5-19* we see where Daniel describes the spirit body of God:

[5] *Then I lifted up mine eyes, and looked, and behold a certain man clothed in linen, whose loins were girded with fine gold of Uphaz:*

[6] *His body also was like the beryl, and his face as the appearance of lightning, and his eyes as lamps of fire, and his arms and his feet like in colour to polished brass, and the voice of his words like the voice of a multitude.*

[7] *And I Daniel alone saw the vision: for the men that were with me saw not the vision; but a great quaking fell upon them, so that they fled to hide themselves.*

[8] *Therefore I was left alone, and saw this great vision, and there remained no strength in me: for my comeliness was turned in me into corruption, and I retained no strength.*

[9] *Yet heard I the voice of his words: and when I heard the voice of his words, then was I in a deep sleep on my face, and my face toward the ground.*

[10] *And, behold, an hand touched me, which set me upon my knees and upon the palms of my hands.*

[11] *And he said unto me, O Daniel, a man greatly beloved, understand the words that I speak unto thee, and stand upright: for unto thee am I now sent. And when he had spoken this word unto me, I stood trembling.*

¹² Then said he unto me, Fear not, Daniel: for from the first day that thou didst set thine heart to understand, and to chasten thyself before thy God, thy words were heard, and I am come for thy words.

¹³ But the prince of the kingdom of Persia withstood me one and twenty days: but, lo, Michael, one of the chief princes, came to help me; and I remained there with the kings of Persia.

¹⁴ Now I am come to make thee understand what shall befall thy people in the latter days: for yet the vision is for many days.

¹⁵ And when he had spoken such words unto me, I set my face toward the ground, and I became dumb.

¹⁶ And, behold, one like the similitude of the sons of men touched my lips: then I opened my mouth, and spake, and said unto him that stood before me, O my lord, by the vision my sorrows are turned upon me, and I have retained no strength.

¹⁷ For how can the servant of this my lord talk with this my lord? for as for me, straightway there remained no strength in me, neither is there breath left in me.

¹⁸ Then there came again and touched me one like the appearance of a man, and he strengthened me,

¹⁹ And said, O man greatly beloved, fear not: peace be unto thee, be strong, yea, be strong. And when he had spoken unto me, I was strengthened, and said, Let my lord speak; for thou hast strengthened me. KJV

Philippians 2:5-7 shows the shape of God, which is the image and likeness of a man:

⁵ Let this mind be in you, which was also in Christ Jesus:

⁶ Who, being in the form of God, thought it not robbery to be equal with God:

⁷ But made himself of no reputation, and took upon him the form of a servant, and was made in the likeness of men:

God also has a personal soul that can display grief, anger, jealousy, hate, pity, pleasure, and delight. God has a personal spirit with mind and intelligence. All of these attributes are also in us.

To better understand how we live, we must first note that **we exist both naturally and spiritually.** There is a spiritual world and a material world. We, as spirit beings, live in the material world (the world in which we can see, touch and smell), but we must not forget that we are spirits having a natural experience. *Hebrews 11:3* states:

> "Through faith we understand that the worlds were framed by the word of God, so that things which are seen were not made of things which do appear."

Everything that we see was made or created by what we cannot see. Notice in this scripture it states that the "worlds" were framed. The letter "s" being on the end of the word "world" indicates that there is more than one world. We have the world of the unseen in which we were created and the world that we can see in which we live in daily.

So, how then were the worlds framed out of nothing? *Hebrews 11:1* states: "Now faith is the substance of things hoped for, the evidence of things not seen." Here we see that faith is called a substance, and through faith, **a substance that cannot be seen with the physical eye, created what we can see with our physical eyes.** In the earlier chapter, we learned that most of the physical parts of us are governed by our experiences, emotions, what we think, etc., which can also be known as physical things. However, when we are talking about the spiritual realm, the other world in which we exist, we are to operate and function by something we cannot see, and that is faith.

How do we get faith? *Romans 12:3* states:

> "For I say, through the grace given unto me, to every man that is among you, not to think of himself more highly than he ought to think; but to think soberly, according as God hath dealt to every man the measure of faith."

This scripture indicates that God has given every man THE measure of faith. God gave everyone, after they were born again, a measure of faith. You believed by faith when you accepted Jesus as your savior that you have now been redeemed from anything that the material world can throw your way. When you made Jesus the Lord of your life the spirit of God immediately moved into your heart. This means now you are expected to live from the inside out. We are now to live by, depend on, and trust in what now resides in us and that is the spirit of the living God. *Ephesians 2:8* states: "For by grace are ye saved through faith; and that not of yourselves: it is the gift of God." Salvation is a gift from God, and because you cannot physically see God, you must believe by faith that you are now saved. ***Faith is also a gift that was given to us by God to keep.***

5

Soteria

Let's take one minute before we continue to talk about faith and go over this word salvation. I want to give you the opportunity before we go any further to say a prayer if you have not done so already in order to better understand how to live from the inside out and this powerful gift called faith.   The Greek word for salvation is *soteria*, which means protection, provision, wealth, wisdom, soundness, and health, total life prosperity. We often look at the word prosperity and think of money. However, it is way more than that. We were originally created to have authority to rule in the earth as God's children, but through the disobedience of Adam, we lost that authority to dominate. Therefore, God had to send Jesus His son, who was born through the Virgin Mary, to come and save what had been lost because we were all heading straight to hell as a result of the fall of Adam. The bible states that we were in Adam.

Therefore, what affected him fell on us even though we were not born yet. It is the same way when a woman is pregnant. She must watch what she puts into her body because she has a baby inside of her, and her diet will affect the unborn child as well as her.

John 3:16 states: "God so loved the world that he gave His only begotten Son, that whosoever believes in Him shall not perish but have everlasting life." Jesus was sent to save us from destruction and being hell bound. *John 3:17* "For God did not send the son into the world to judge the world but the world shall be saved through him." Therefore, it is important that we all be saved; **whoever calls upon the Name of the Lord shall be saved.**

Please read this prayer out loud:

> "Father, I come to you now just as I am. You know my life. You know how I have lived. Forgive me, Lord. I repent of my sins. I believe that Jesus died, and on the third day, He rose so that I can be free. Now, Father, I ask that you live your life in me and through me from this day forth. I now belong to you. In Jesus' name, I am now saved!"

That is it! God now lives in your heart. You should be so excited because now you will read the rest of this book and get revelation from God because He lives inside of you. Welcome to the family of Christ! Your life will never be the same in Jesus' name.

Galatians 2:20 states:

> "I am crucified with Christ: nevertheless I live; yet not I, but Christ liveth in me: and the life which I now live in

the flesh I live by the faith of the Son of God, who loved
me, and gave himself for me."

By saying that prayer, you understand that although you are housed
in the flesh, you are nothing without God and the life you now live, you
live by faith. Faith has now been born into your heart. The measure of
faith that you have now received is enough to do whatever you want
with it, according to the plans that God has for your life. We will talk
more about faith later in the book.

6

The Spiritual World

Let's take a look at the two worlds in which we exist. **We have a spiritual world and a material world.** In *John 3* in the amplified bible, we find Nicodemus who was a leader among the Jews. He came to Jesus and stated in verse 2:

> "We know and are certain that You have come from God [as] a Teacher; for no one can do these signs (these wonderworks, these miracles—and produce the proofs) that You do unless God is with him."

Jesus answered him:

> "I assure you, most solemnly I tell you, that unless a person is born again (anew, from above), he cannot ever see (know, be acquainted with, and experience) the kingdom of God."

In the previous chapter, you prayed the salvation prayer, which automatically qualified you as being "born again," also known as "born from above." This means now we are different and have additional tools that can be utilized than those who are not born again. We know we are in the world but not of it. This means that we are operating from another dimension. We don't fully operate from the seen realm. We also have access to the realm of the unseen.

You may be wondering how does one live from a world that we cannot see and where is this world located? In Luke 17, the Pharisees posed a question to Jesus about the coming of the kingdom of God. Jesus answered by saying in verses 20 and 21:

> "The kingdom of God cometh not with observation: Neither shall they say, Lo here! or, lo there! for, behold, the kingdom of God is within you."

After studying this verse for many years, I finally got the revelation that ***as soon as I was born again/born from above, I was changed from the inside.*** I was immediately given some new birthrights. All of my rights are now in line with what Jesus has already done for me. In Luke 17, Jesus explained to the Pharisees that ***the kingdom is not a location, it is within you.*** Before we were born again, we were limited to living by the things of the material world, but now that we have chosen Jesus as our Lord and savior, we are to live now by another system, which is the Kingdom of God.

7

Kingdom of God

What is the Kingdom of God? **The Kingdom of God is a culture.** Culture is defined as the characteristics of a particular group of people. The Kingdom of God is a theocracy, not a democracy. A theocracy has only one ruler, and in the Kingdom, GOD is the ONLY ruler. In the material world, the rules are based on a majority of people voting to establish the rules and regulations. As Christians, we do not get a vote in the Kingdom of God. We are to do things the way God intends for us to do them. God sent Jesus as an example of the way we should live while living in the material world. *Matthew 6:33: "But seek ye first the kingdom of God, and his righteousness; and all these things shall be added unto you."* Another translation states to seek the way that God does things. This means that we are to live the way God (who is king of this kingdom) would live. **The Kingdom of God is a spiritual reality.** It is spiritual because it is a culture of its own that is shaped by a king who is a spirit. Remember in a previous chapter, we stated that we are a spirit that is made in the image of God. Therefore, the real we, which are spirit, have now been born into a different culture when we accepted Christ as our personal savior. We must understand that we are not from Earth. ***We are from heaven, and we came to Earth to bring the spiritual kingdom concept to Earth by manifesting it from the inside out.***

When we became a part of the kingdom culture, we received a benefit package. We found our benefit plan in the word of God.

We were immediately given angels to watch over us and keep us safe. *Luke 4:10.* God promises that He will take care of us. *Matthew 6.* God promises us peace, joy, and to be in right standing with Him even when things are not looking as we think they should in our lives. *Romans 14:17.* He has taken all of our heavy burdens and has given us Jesus' yoke, which is easy and His burden, which is light. *Matthew 11:3* This means that we never have to carry anything heavy on our own. It doesn't matter if it is an addiction, wrong thinking patterns, stress, etc. Jesus has already taken care of those issues on the cross. Therefore, we must learn to cast those cares over on Him.

In the Kingdom, God has promised us long life. In *Psalms 91,* he promised that He would give us long life and show us His salvation. We defined salvation in the earlier chapters. God has made a promise to let us live long enough so that we may experience total prosperity. This means in our health, relationships, bank accounts, etc. *2 Corinthians 4:4*

> "In whom the god of this world hath blinded the minds of them which believe not, lest the light of the glorious gospel of Christ, who is the image of God, should shine unto them."

We can see from the scripture that the god of this world—the god that governs the system of this world who is satan— has blinded the minds in order for people not to believe. Therefore, many do not believe that they should have total prosperity, which means nothing missing or nothing broken. They believe in struggling, lack, and sickness, etc., because that has been accepted as the norm in the material world.

2 Corinthians 10:5 states:

> "Casting **down** imaginations, and **every high thing** that exalteth itself against the knowledge of God, and bringing into captivity every thought to the obedience of Christ"

This is teaching us that we are to cast away or get rid of things that are not in line with Christ. The "high" thing that is spoken of in this scripture is what the world believes. People who are not saved tend to go with what is popular. In other words, a few people die of what you have been diagnosed with. Do you believe what happened to them will happen to you? Or do you believe the word as it pertains to your healing? The "high" thing (the way the world thinks) must be cast out with the word of God! You must release out of your mouth: "I am healed." No matter how you feel, you must believe that you are healed. The bible states that "by His stripes WE WERE healed" and by His stripes WE ARE healed. That means it is already done, and the only way to see it manifest in your life is to believe it.

8

Grace

God has given us grace as kingdom citizens. Grace is defined as unmerited favor. This is something that we obtain a right to as born again Christians. We don't have to work for our benefit plan. We just believe that we have it.

1 Corinthians 15:10 [amplied] :

> "But by the grace of God I am what I am: and his grace which was bestowed upon me was not in vain; but I laboured more abundantly than they all: yet not I, but the grace of God which was with me."

Grace is a gift that came through Christ. In order to operate in it, we must understand the law that governs grace. It does not require "works." Most people feel as though they need to work for grace because it is hard for the mind to understand how they can receive something that they did not earn or deserve. The spiritual world does not work the same way the material world works. For example, when a person starts a new job, they have to work a certain number of hours before they can start vacation or take any time off. In the kingdom, we have a law that will connect us to the benefit plan immediately, and that is the law of faith. *Romans 3:27:* "Where is boasting then? It is excluded. By what law? of works? Nay: but by the law of faith."

9

Laws of the Kingdom

In the material world, we have laws that we must live by. This is also true in the Kingdom of God. ***In the kingdom we must live by faith.*** Faith gives us access to our kingdom benefit plan. When the law of faith is violated, we punish ourselves by not operating in the fullness of the kingdom. In the material world, our constitution requires freedom and justice for all material world citizens. However, if a law is broken, freedom and justice are limited while time is being served for the law that has been broken, which is also known as a crime.

In the kingdom, when we don't believe or have faith, we have limited our supply of receiving from God due to our unbelief. We will find in four different areas in the word of God where God has called us to live by faith. *Habakkuk 2:4, Romans 1:17, Galatians 3:11,* and

Hebrews 10:38. These four scriptures are commands from God in how we should live.

Hebrews 11:6:

> "But without faith it is impossible to please him: for he that cometh to God must believe that he is, and that he is a rewarder of them that diligently seek him."

This scripture states that we are rewarded when we believe.

Faith or belief in the spiritual world is also known as the conception process. We must see the substance of a thing in the spirit before we can see it materialize. When a baby is conceived in a mother's womb, we don't see it at first, but we believe it is there. After confirmation has been given of this substance that we cannot see, several months later that substance is then birthed from the unseen realm into the natural realm. This is also true with faith. You believe that you have that job even though you cannot see it. However, faith will produce that job as long as you continue to believe.

When is it appropriate to use our faith? Let's take another look at *Hebrews 11:1.* It states "Now faith." This means that as kingdom citizens, we are never to leave faith. Faith is always now.

Mark 11:24:

> "Therefore I say unto you, What things soever ye desire, when ye pray, believe that ye receive them, and ye shall have them."

This scripture is stating that we are to believe that we have what we are praying for when? NOW! When we leave faith, we are in violation of the law that governs the kingdom. When we don't believe, we cannot receive. The word *FAITH* is: *Full Assurance In That Happening.* No wavering, no doubting only believe.

10

The Voice of Faith

Genesis 1:3: "And God said, 'Let there be light,' and there was light." Notice in this scripture that when God saw darkness upon the earth, He did not sit back and think, 'Wow, it sure is dark around here.' Instead, He knew that when He spoke, something would change. We are to live the same way. Faith has a voice, and as we see in the spiritual realm what we would like to see in the material/natural realm, we are to speak it out of our mouths into the atmosphere and allow faith to produce it. It is not necessary to stand around and try to figure out how it will come to pass; that is the awesome thing about kingdom principles. If there is something additional for you to do, God will give instructions; however, when you have done all you can do, you stand by faith.

The voice of faith can be compared to putting a key in a car ignition. Without turning the key, the car will not travel to the desired destination. When operating by the law of faith, if we do not open our mouths and speak, we are not allowing our faith to be put into motion. The bible encourages us in *Romans 4:17* to speak those things that are not as though they were. Changing the material world with the voice of faith is a privilege that we have in the body of Christ.

11

Fear

Fear is the root of the world's operation. The material world is built on survival, which means barely making it. In the kingdom, we are considered more than conquerors, which means not only do we thrive; we are victorious. In the material world, people try to survive or live by doing things the way they want to do them. The enemy has set the material world's operation on buying, selling, greed, wealth, lust, and fame, all of which are temporary operations. The United States government remains in a deficit, which means they will always be a servant to the lender. With this type of system in operation, there is no certainty where the economy will end up. And for those who depend on this type of system, they are subject to remain in fear because there are no promises or grantees. Some things in the world system will work for a while. However, anything that is done outside of the way God intended for us to do them will not last. It will come to an end.

Fear is designed to paralyze progress while faith is designed to keep us moving forward no matter how we feel. Fear and faith are totally opposite operations. I have heard some people state that it is important to have some fear to stay alive. I totally disagree with that. The only fear that we should have is the fear that is defined in the word of God, which is the total reverence and respect for God. I think some often get fear and wisdom confused. For example, I cannot swim. If someone invites me over to a pool party, I will not participate in any activity that requires me to swim. This does not make me afraid of water; it simply means that since I cannot swim, I will not dive into the pool.

The bible states in Proverbs that wisdom is the principle thing. Faith, on the other hand, is used when you are on the boat, and the boat begins to sink; even though you cannot swim, you say I am not going down. You have faith that you will not drown because you remember the promises of God, which say that although I find myself in a dangerous situation, I will trust the word of God that He will never leave me or forsake me.

Faith keeps you alive when everything else around you appears to be dead. *Luke 8:43-48* ^{The message bible}

> In the crowd that day there was a woman who for twelve years had been afflicted with hemorrhages. She had spent every penny she had on doctors but not one had been able to help her. She slipped in from behind and touched

the edge of Jesus' robe. At that very moment her hemorrhaging stopped. Jesus said, "Who touched me?"

When no one stepped forward, Peter said, "But Master, we've got crowds of people on our hands. Dozens have touched you."

[46]Jesus insisted, "Someone touched me. I felt power discharging from me."

[47]When the woman realized that she couldn't remain hidden, she knelt trembling before him. In front of all the people, she blurted out her story—why she touched him and how at that same moment she was healed.

[48]Jesus said, "Daughter, you took a risk trusting me, and now you're healed and whole. Live well, live blessed!"

This lady had this issue for twelve years and had been told that there was nothing that could be done about it. Instead of looking forward to her death, she trusted that she could be healed and she was. In verse 46, Jesus stated that He felt power discharging from Him. That power that He is referring to is her faith. Her faith put a demand on healing virtue to come from the healer into her body immediately. The lady was operating in NOW faith. She was determined to operate from the inside out. She believed first in her heart that she did not have to live the rest of her life in the condition that she was in, and she was able to receive her healing.

Being in the kingdom of God, we must leave our senses and operate from the inside where all of our help comes from. Faith will never make sense because faith is not connected to our flesh. It is a spiritual concept that requires obedience and trust in God. Faith is designed to produce things. God told Noah that he needed to build an ark because it was going to rain for several days, and without the ark, the animals and people would not survive. Noah had to trust God and do what He said. At the time, there was no rain expected for several days. If Noah had taken the time to try to rationalize what God was saying, he may have never completed the assignment. Ask yourself, have you completed the assignment that God has given you? Do you even know what that assignment is?

Let's take a look at another part of faith that we must use if we want to see results of what we are believing God for.

12

Sowing and Reaping

In *Mark 4:14*[King James] we find a parable that states "the sower soweth the word." In the New Living Translation, it states, "The farmer plants seed by taking God's word to others." As kingdom citizens, we are the farmers who sow and eventually reap a harvest. The world system of buying and selling totally depends on the economy for its harvest. In *Luke 8:11*, we find that "the seed is the word of God." Therefore, we plant seed (the word of God) not only by being hearers of the word but also by being doers as well. There have been great criticisms regarding giving to the poor or to the local church. Most people feel that it is the government's responsibility to meet the needs of the poor. It is the responsibility of the body of Christ to take care of the poor. There isn't a scripture in the bible where you will find Jesus looking for a king or president to help feed, clothe, or house the poor. To me, it is almost like debating with a dictionary after looking up a word and reading the definition. If you are seeking a source to gain clarity, you must believe that the source is accurate. Therefore, when we read the bible, and it tells us to "sow the word," which we have learned that we are to do, it says there should not be any room for speculation; it is written, therefore, adhere to the instructions.

The word of God is also known as incorruptible seed. Incorruptible means that it is everlasting; it will never cease to exist. No matter how many laws and leaders change in the world, the word of God will always remain the same and have the same power from the day it was originally written.

Sowing and reaping is a law in the kingdom of God, and it is also known as seedtime and harvest. In the material world, if you work for the same business, everyone usually gets paid or receives wages for their labor on the same day. However, in the kingdom, our seedtime and harvest is personalized by God. In *Ecclesiastes 3*, you will find a clear breakdown of seasons and timing. We can all agree that we all were not born on the same day and neither will we all leave Earth on the same day. Why? Because God has individualized us according to His purpose and His plans for our lives. Therefore, we will not all receive our harvest at the same time.

What then is a law and how does this law of sowing and reaping work in the kingdom of God? Well, I am glad you asked. A law is defined in *Webster's Dictionary* as:

"a statement of fact, deduced from observation, to the effect that a particular natural or scientific phenomenon always occurs if certain conditions are present."

In *Genesis 8-22*, we find the conditions that need to be present for this law to be a factual statement.

"While the earth remaineth, seedtime and harvest, and cold and heat, and summer and winter, and day and night shall not cease."

We can all arrive at the conclusion that all of the seasons listed in this promise from God yet exist; therefore, seedtime and harvest is a law that can be in full operation in your life if you believe in God's promises. ***Always remember that faith is the password to receiving all of the promises of God.***

The seed (the word of God) that we sow determines what we receive. The Kingdom of God is symbolic of planting or casting seed into the ground. *Mark 4:26-32* Amplified Bible (AMP)

[26] And He said, The kingdom of God is like a man who scatters seed upon the ground, [27] And then continues sleeping and rising night and day while the seed sprouts and grows and [a] increases—he knows not how.

[28] The earth produces [acting] by itself—first the blade, then the ear, then the full grain in the ear.

[29] But when the grain is ripe and permits, immediately he [b] sends forth [the reapers] and puts in the sickle, because the harvest stands ready.

[30] And He said, With what can we compare the kingdom of God, or what parable shall we use to illustrate and explain it?

³¹ It is like a grain of mustard seed, which, when sown upon the ground, is the smallest of all seeds upon the earth;

³² Yet after it is sown, it grows up and becomes the greatest of all garden herbs and puts out large branches, so that the birds of the air are able to make nests and dwell in its shade.

13

Ambassadors

Not all are called to be leaders in ministry. Christians have a tendency to believe that just because they know the word of God and have been able to minister to a few of the saints, they should be a pastor or apostle, etc. They then call a meeting with their pastor and say that they are "called," and the next thing you know, the pastor has a ceremony and places a title in front of their name, and now they are a prophetess or evangelist, etc. Most of the time, the pastor goes along with this for fear of losing that person as a member of their church. This foolishness MUST stop. We are NOT all called to the fivefold ministry because we know the word. The bible states in *Ephesians 4: 11-12*:

> [11] And he gave some, apostles; and some, prophets; and some, evangelists; and some, pastors and teacher;
> [12] For the perfecting of the saints, for the work of the ministry, for the edifying of the body of Christ:

The key to this scripture is in the first line that says "He" gave. Some of us have given ourselves titles, and that is why some of the communities in which we live in appear as though God is not among us. Just because you are not a leader in the church does not mean you do not have an assignment. We all have an assignment as Christian people to invade darkness on Earth with kingdom light. To accomplish that, we must spend time with God to get our marching orders and in the area in which He has sent us.

It is important that we understand that we all have an assignment in the kingdom. We have talked about not being from here and having our own culture. We are to bring the way God wants things done on Earth from the spiritual world into the natural world. By doing this, we are considered ambassadors. ***Ambassadors are people who are sent to represent or promote something.*** In this case, we are sent to the earth to promote the kingdom of God and show others who they are and the original plan and purpose that God has for their lives. *2 Corinthians 5:16-20* Message Bible

> **16-20** "Because of this decision we don't evaluate people by what they have or how they look. We looked at the Messiah that way once and got it all wrong, as you know. We certainly don't look at him that way anymore. Now we look inside, and what we see is that anyone united with the Messiah gets a fresh start, is created new. The old life is gone; a new life burgeons! Look at it! All this comes from the God who settled the relationship between us and him, and then called us to settle our relationships with each other. God put the world square with himself through the

Messiah, giving the world a fresh start by offering forgiveness of sins. God has given us the task of telling everyone what he is doing. We're Christ's representatives. God uses us to persuade men and women to drop their differences and enter into God's work of making things right between them. We're speaking for Christ himself now: Become friends with God; he's already a friend with you."

We are not sent here to blend in or to take sides. *We are sent here to take authority over everything that is operating outside of the original way that God intended things to be.* We are not here to represent our nationalities or gender and to debate if we are Hebrews or of an African descent, etc., but to represent the love of Christ and seek to help those who are lost. If you consider yourself an ambassador for Christ, you should never find yourself being loyal to things that the world uses to cause division or strife. We are to use the word of God as our tool for success.

In the material world, the federal government regulates how we live. The federal government has three parts: the *executive branch* to enforce the laws, the *legislative branch* to create the laws, and the *judicial branch* to hear cases and seek justice.

In the spiritual world, there is only one government, and unlike the three branches of government with headquarters in Washington, DC, this government is located on the shoulders of Jesus Christ. *Isaiah 9:6* God knew that because of the fall of Adam and his giving the authority of the earth over to satan through Adam's disobedience, there would be some flaws in the world's way of governing the earth. So He sent Jesus as a representative on Earth to bring forth a flawless government that would take mankind back to its original state. This form of government simply means that the responsibility of rules, judgment, and justice is upon Him. Again, this is going to require that we believe that there is a system that is far more powerful than the system that is in the material world. This does not mean that we do not have to keep the material world's laws. After all, we are in the world even though we are not from here. However, as kingdom citizens any laws that are made that are not lined up with the word of God we can prohibit them in prayer.

14

Pillars

We have seven pillars (kingdoms) that operate in the world. We have religion, family, education, government, media, arts/entertainment /sports, and business. Most of the time, you will find that the "god" of this world (satan) has strategically placed his people in leadership positions in these 7 kingdoms in order to have authority over them. We would like to believe that Christians would at least be in charge of the pillar of religion, but that isn't so. Many religious leaders are leading people straight to hell by using false teachings and implementing their own way of doing things and leaving God out of their plans than ever before. That is why it is up to us as ambassadors not only to rely on the leadership of the church to take authority and help those that are lost but also to take responsibility to find out what pillar we are called to and take dominion in that area.

God has already gifted you with everything you need inside of you to make a difference in the area you are called to. We all started off as a seed in the womb of our mother. Inside of us from the very beginning was purpose. It is as simple as asking Him, "What is my purpose in life?" It is also important to be a member of a church that is teaching the word of God with demonstration. This means that you can see the word of God working in the leader's personal lives as well as the ministry. At the same time, signs, wonders, and miracles are taking place, and people are getting revelation from the teachings and returning with testimonies.

I remember attending my church over ten years ago. God spoke to me during the service about starting a program that houses men who are coming out of prison. With no criminal background, I had no idea why I would do this. As I continued to listen and obey, everything started to come together. I have been able to house over eighty-eight men in my transitional housing program while providing wraparound services to them to help reduce the recidivism rate.

Looking at the different pillars that I have explained, I realized that I had been called to government. We are not only housing the formerly incarcerated; we are also praying and changing laws that are related to those that are affected by incarceration. I go into courtrooms, speak to judges and attorneys, and work on ways to improve treatment of criminals rather than putting them in a jail or prison. God has provided me with avenues to implement programs in the jails and prisons that help people to identify the roots of their incarceration and change those behaviors. I serve as a motivational speaker in facilities to give the incarcerated hope in a hopeless environment. I have kings who hold very high political positions call me and ask for advice.

Wherever you are called, it is important that you leave a mark that cannot be erased. Please do not spend time trying to influence or impress people by your works or words. The bible states that God will bless you and make your name great, and your gift will bring you before great men. God has already gone ahead of you and made all the crooked paths straight. Your angels are already in their proper position and waiting to aid and protect you along the way. So, what are you waiting on? Now that you know who you are and how you should live, let's take the first step and get in our proper positions and invade the material world with light.

Welcome To The Kingdom Of God

Scripture Reference Section for Kingdom Citizens

- Kingdom Identity (Who are you)

- Kingdom Eligibility/Operation (How to become a member of the Kingdom of God)

- Management (GOD)

- Benefits (As Kingdom Citizens)

- Conflict of interest (Faith verses Fear)

- Conduct Standards (Behavior in the Kingdom)

- Affirmative Action (Favor)

- Grievance Procedure (Prayer)

- Compensation (Sowing and Reaping)

Kingdom Identity (Who are you)

2 Corinthians 5:17 ESV / Therefore, if anyone is in Christ, he is a new creation. The old has passed away; behold, the new has come.

1 Peter 2:9 ESV / But you are a chosen race, a royal priesthood, a holy nation, a people for his own possession, that you may proclaim the excellencies of him who called you out of darkness into his marvelous light.

Ephesians 2:10 ESV / For we are his workmanship, created in Christ Jesus for good works, which God prepared beforehand, that we should walk in them.

Romans 8:1 ESV / There is therefore now no condemnation for those who are in Christ Jesus.

John 1:12 ESV / But to all who did receive him, who believed in his name, he gave the right to become children of God

2 Corinthians 5:21 ESV / For our sake he made him to be sin who knew no sin, so that in him we might become the righteousness of God.

1 Corinthians 6:19 ESV / Or do you not know that your body is a temple of the Holy Spirit within you, whom you have from God? You are not your own,

John 15:5 ESV / I am the vine; you are the branches. Whoever abides in me and I in him, he it is that bears much fruit, for apart from me you can do nothing.

Romans 12:2 ESV / Do not be conformed to this world, but be transformed by the renewal of your mind, that by testing you may discern what is the will of God, what is good and acceptable and perfect.

1 John 4:4 ESV / Little children, you are from God and have overcome them, for he who is in you is greater than he who is in the world.

John 15:15 ESV / No longer do I call you servants, for the servant does not know what his master is doing; but I have called you friends, for all that I have heard from my Father I have made known to you.

1 Corinthians 12:27 ESV / Now you are the body of Christ and individually members of it.

Galatians 3:26 ESV / For in Christ Jesus you are all sons of God, through faith.

Philippians 3:20 ESV / But our citizenship is in heaven, and from it we await a Savior, the Lord Jesus Christ,

1 Thessalonians 5:5 ESV / For you are all children of light, children of the day. We are not of the night or of the darkness.

1 Corinthians 3:16 ESV / Do you not know that you are God's temple and that God's Spirit dwells in you?

1 Peter 2:9-10 ESV / But you are a chosen race, a royal priesthood, a holy nation, a people for his own possession, that you may proclaim the excellencies of him who called you out of darkness into his marvelous light. Once you were not a people, but now you are God's people; once you had not received mercy, but now you have received mercy.

Romans 5:1 ESV / Therefore, since we have been justified by faith, we have peace with God through our Lord Jesus Christ.

2 Peter 1:4 ESV / By which he has granted to us his precious and very great promises, so that through them you may become partakers of the divine nature, having escaped from the corruption that is in the world because of sinful desire

1 Corinthians 6:20 ESV / For you were bought with a price. So glorify God in your body.

2 Corinthians 5:20 ESV / Therefore, we are ambassadors for Christ, God making his appeal through us. We implore you on behalf of Christ, be reconciled to God.

Ephesians 2:6 ESV / And raised us up with him and seated us with him in the heavenly places in Christ Jesus,

Romans 6:18 ESV / And, having been set free from sin, have become slaves of righteousness.

Psalm 139:14 ESV / I praise you, for I am fearfully and wonderfully made. Wonderful are your works; my soul knows it very well.

Matthew 5:14 ESV / "You are the light of the world. A city set on a hill cannot be hidden.

Galatians 2:20 ESV / I have been crucified with Christ. It is no longer I who live, but Christ who lives in me. And the life I now live in the flesh I live by faith in the Son of God, who loved me and gave himself for me.

Ephesians 1:7-8 ESV / In him we have redemption through his blood, the forgiveness of our trespasses, according to the riches of his grace, which he lavished upon us, in all wisdom and insight

Colossians 1:13 ESV / He has delivered us from the domain of darkness and transferred us to the kingdom of his beloved Son

1 Corinthians 3:9 ESV / For we are God's fellow workers. You are God's field, God's building.

Galatians 4:6 ESV / And because you are sons, God has sent the Spirit of his Son into our hearts, crying, "Abba! Father!"

John 15:1-5 ESV / "I am the true vine, and my Father is the vinedresser. Every branch in me that does not bear fruit he takes away, and every branch that does bear fruit he prunes, that it may bear more fruit. Already you are clean because of the word that I have spoken to you. Abide in me, and I in you. As the branch cannot bear fruit by itself, unless it abides in the vine, neither can you, unless you abide in me. I am the vine; you are the branches. Whoever abides in me and I in him, he it is that bears much fruit, for apart from me you can do nothing.

Romans 8:17 ESV / And if children, then heirs—heirs of God and fellow heirs with Christ, provided we suffer with him in order that we may also be glorified with him.

Colossians 3:3 ESV / For you have died, and your life is hidden with Christ in God.

Ephesians 3:12 ESV / In whom we have boldness and access with confidence through our faith in him.

1 Corinthians 12:13 ESV / For in one Spirit we were all baptized into one body—Jews or Greeks, slaves or free—and all were made to drink of one Spirit

Matthew 5:13 ESV / "You are the salt of the earth, but if salt has lost its taste, how shall its saltiness be restored? It is no longer good for anything except to be thrown out and trampled under people's feet.

Kingdom Eligibility/ Operation (How to Become a Member of the Kingdom of God)

2 Corinthians 5:17 ESV / Therefore, if anyone is in Christ, he is a new creation. The old has passed away; behold, the new has come.

1 Corinthians 6:11 ESV / And such were some of you. But you were washed, you were sanctified, you were justified in the name of the Lord Jesus Christ and by the Spirit of our God.

1 Corinthians 6:9 ESV / Or do you not know that the unrighteous will not inherit the kingdom of God? Do not be deceived: neither the sexually immoral, nor idolaters, nor adulterers, nor men who practice homosexuality.

Hebrews 11:6 ESV / And without faith it is impossible to please him, for whoever would draw near to God must believe that he exists and that he rewards those who seek him.

Mark 11:22-24 ESV / And Jesus answered them, "Have faith in God. Truly, I say to you, whoever says to this mountain, 'Be taken up and thrown into the sea,' and does not doubt in his heart, but believes that what he says will come to pass, it will be done for him. Therefore I tell you, whatever you ask in prayer, believe that you have received it, and it will be yours.

James 2:24 ESV / You see that a person is justified by works and not by faith alone.

2 Corinthians 5:7 ESV / For we walk by faith, not by sight.

James 1:5-8 ESV / If any of you lacks wisdom, let him ask God, who gives generously to all without reproach, and it will be given him. But let him ask in faith, with no doubting, for the one who doubts is like a wave of the sea that is driven and tossed by the wind. For that person must not suppose that he will receive anything from the Lord; he is a double-minded man, unstable in all his ways.

Hebrews 11:7 ESV / By faith Noah, being warned by God concerning events as yet unseen, in reverent fear constructed an ark for the saving of his household. By this he condemned the world and became an heir of the righteousness that comes by faith.

Galatians 2:16 ESV / Yet we know that a person is not justified by works of the law but through faith in Jesus Christ, so we also have believed in Christ Jesus, in order to be justified by faith in Christ and not by works of the law, because by works of the law no one will be justified.

Matthew 21:21-22 ESV / And Jesus answered them, "Truly, I say to you, if you have faith and do not doubt, you will not only do what has been done to the fig tree, but even if you say to this mountain, 'Be taken up and thrown into the sea,' it will happen. And whatever you ask in prayer, you will receive, if you have faith."

Philippians 4:13 ESV / I can do all things through him who strengthens me.

James 2:18 ESV / But someone will say, "You have faith and I have works." Show me your faith apart from your works, and I will show you my faith by my works.

Proverbs 3:6 ESV / In all your ways acknowledge him, and he will make straight your paths.

Romans 5:1-5 ESV / Therefore, since we have been justified by faith, we have peace with God through our Lord Jesus Christ. Through him we have also obtained access by faith into this grace in which we stand, and we rejoice in hope of the glory of God. More than that, we rejoice in our sufferings, knowing that suffering produces endurance, and endurance produces character, and character produces hope, and hope does not put us to shame, because God's love has been poured into our hearts through the Holy Spirit who has been given to us.

1 Timothy 6:12 ESV / Fight the good fight of the faith. Take hold of the eternal life to which you were called and about which you made the good confession in the presence of many witnesses.

Mark 11:22 ESV / And Jesus answered them, "Have faith in God.

Luke 18:27 ESV / But he said, "What is impossible with men is possible with God."

Kingdom Management (God)

1 Timothy 2:5 ESV / For there is one God, and there is one mediator between God and men, the man Christ Jesus,

Isaiah 44:6 ESV / Thus says the Lord, the King of Israel and his Redeemer, the Lord of hosts: "I am the first and I am the last; besides me there is no god.

Isaiah 43:11 ESV / I, I am the Lord, and besides me there is no savior.

1 Corinthians 8:6 ESV / Yet for us there is one God, the Father, from whom are all things and for whom we exist, and one Lord, Jesus Christ, through whom are all things and through whom we exist.

James 2:19 ESV / You believe that God is one; you do well. Even the demons believe—and shudder!

Revelation 1:8 ESV / "I am the Alpha and the Omega," says the Lord God, "who is and who was and who is to come, the Almighty."

Isaiah 42:8 ESV / I am the Lord; that is my name; my glory I give to no other, nor my praise to carved idols.

Colossians 1:16 ESV / For by him all things were created, in heaven and on earth, visible and invisible, whether thrones or dominions or rulers or authorities—all things were created through him and for him.

John 1:1 ESV / In the beginning was the Word, and the Word was with God, and the Word was God.

Isaiah 44:24 ESV / Thus says the Lord, your Redeemer, who formed you from the womb: "I am the Lord, who made all things, who alone stretched out the heavens, who spread out the earth by myself,

<u>Ephesians 4:5</u> ESV / One Lord, one faith, one baptism,

<u>John 4:24</u> ESV / God is spirit, and those who worship him must worship in spirit and truth."

<u>John 1:14</u> ESV / And the Word became flesh and dwelt among us, and we have seen his glory, glory as of the only Son from the Father, full of grace and truth.

<u>Exodus 20:3</u> ESV / "You shall have no other gods before me."

Benefits
(As Kingdom Citizens)

1 John 1:7 ESV / But if we walk in the light, as he is in the light, we have fellowship with one another, and the blood of Jesus his Son cleanses us from all sin.

Ephesians 1:7 ESV / In him we have redemption through his blood, the forgiveness of our trespasses, according to the riches of his grace,

Galatians 2:20 ESV / I have been crucified with Christ. It is no longer I who live, but Christ who lives in me. And the life I now live in the flesh I live by faith in the Son of God, who loved me and gave himself for me.

Romans 8:31 ESV / What then shall we say to these things? If God is for us, who can be against us?

Psalm 103:2-5 ESV / Bless the Lord, O my soul, and forget not all his benefits, who forgives all your iniquity, who heals all your diseases, who redeems your life from the pit, who crowns you with steadfast love and mercy, who satisfies you with good so that your youth is renewed like the eagle's.

Isaiah 41:10 ESV / Fear not, for I am with you; be not dismayed, for I am your God; I will strengthen you, I will help you, I will uphold you with my righteous right hand.

Isaiah 53:5 ESV / But he was wounded for our transgressions; he was crushed for our iniquities; upon him was the chastisement that brought us peace, and with his stripes we are healed.

Psalm 103:2-4 ESV / Bless the Lord, O my soul, and forget not all his benefits, who forgives all your iniquity, who heals all your diseases, who redeems your life from the pit, who crowns you with steadfast love and mercy,

James 5:15 ESV / And the prayer of faith will save the one who is sick, and the Lord will raise him up. And if he has committed sins, he will be forgiven.

James 5:16 ESV / Therefore, confess your sins to one another and pray for one another, that you may be healed. The prayer of a righteous person has great power as it is working.

3 John 1:2 ESV / Beloved, I pray that all may go well with you and that you may be in good health, as it goes well with your soul.

Psalm 147:3 ESV / He heals the brokenhearted and binds up their wounds.

Philippians 4:19 ESV / And my God will supply every need of yours according to his riches in glory in Christ Jesus.

Isaiah 54:17 ESV / "No weapon that is fashioned against you shall succeed, and you shall confute every tongue that rises against you in judgment. This is the heritage of the servants of the Lord and their vindication from me, declares the Lord."

Matthew 11:28 ESV / Come to me, all who labor and are heavy laden, and I will give you rest.

2 Corinthians 12:9 ESV / But he said to me, "My grace is sufficient for you, for my power is made perfect in weakness." Therefore I will boast all the more gladly of my weaknesses, so that the power of Christ may rest upon me.

James 4:7 ESV / Submit yourselves therefore to God. Resist the devil, and he will flee from you.

Philippians 4:6-7 ESV / Do not be anxious about anything, but in everything by prayer and supplication with thanksgiving let your requests be made known to God. And the peace of God, which surpasses all understanding, will guard your hearts and your minds in Christ Jesus.

Proverbs 3:5-8 ESV / Trust in the Lord with all your heart, and do not lean on your own understanding. In all your ways acknowledge him, and he will make straight your paths. Be not wise in your own eyes; fear the Lord, and turn away from evil. It will be healing to your flesh and refreshment to your bones.

John 14:27 ESV / Peace I leave with you; my peace I give to you. Not as the world gives do I give to you. Let not your hearts be troubled, neither let them be afraid.

Psalm 107:20 ESV / "He sent out his word and healed them, and delivered them from their destruction.

Luke 10:19-20 ESV / "Behold, I have given you authority to tread on serpents and scorpions, and over all the power of the enemy, and nothing shall hurt you. Nevertheless, do not rejoice in this, that the spirits are subject to you, but rejoice that your names are written in heaven."

Conflict of Interest
(Faith versus Fear)

Romans 10:17 ESV / So faith comes from hearing, and hearing through the word of Christ.

Hebrews 11:6 ESV / And without faith it is impossible to please him, for whoever would draw near to God must believe that he exists and that he rewards those who seek him.

Matthew 21:22 ESV / "And whatever you ask in prayer, you will receive, if you have faith."

Mark 11:22-24 ESV / And Jesus answered them, "Have faith in God. Truly, I say to you, whoever says to this mountain, 'Be taken up and thrown into the sea,' and does not doubt in his heart, but believes that what he says will come to pass, it will be done for him. Therefore I tell you, whatever you ask in prayer, believe that you have received it, and it will be yours.

Luke 1:37 ESV / For nothing will be impossible with God.

Hebrews 11:1 ESV / Now faith is the assurance of things hoped for, the conviction of things not seen.

Hebrews 11:1-13:25 ESV / Now faith is the assurance of things hoped for, the conviction of things not seen. For by it the people of old received their commendation. By faith we understand that the universe was created by the word of God, so that what is seen was not made out of things that are visible. By faith Abel offered to God a more acceptable sacrifice than Cain, through which he was commended as righteous, God commending him by accepting his gifts. And through his faith, though he died, he still speaks. By faith Enoch was taken up so that he should not see death, and he was not found, because God had taken him. Now before he was taken he was commended as having pleased God. ...

Ephesians 2:8 ESV / For by grace you have been saved through faith. And this is not your own doing; it is the gift of God,

1 Corinthians 2:5 ESV / That your faith might not rest in the wisdom of men but in the power of God.

2 Corinthians 5:7 ESV / For we walk by faith, not by sight

James 1:5-8 ESV / If any of you lacks wisdom, let him ask God, who gives generously to all without reproach, and it will be given him. But let him ask in faith, with no doubting, for the one who doubts is like a wave of the sea that is driven and tossed by the wind. For that person must not suppose that he will receive anything from the Lord; he is a double-minded man, unstable in all his ways.

Hebrews 11:7 ESV / By faith Noah, being warned by God concerning events as yet unseen, in reverent fear constructed an ark for the saving of his household. By this he condemned the world and became an heir of the righteousness that comes by faith.

Philippians 4:13 ESV / I can do all things through him who strengthens me.

Romans 4:20-21 ESV / No distrust made him waver concerning the promise of God, but he grew strong in his faith as he gave glory to God, fully convinced that God was able to do what he had promised.

Habakkuk 2:4 ESV / "Behold, his soul is puffed up; it is not upright within him, but the righteous shall live by his faith.

Romans 5:1-5 ESV / Therefore, since we have been justified by faith, we have peace with God through our Lord Jesus Christ. Through him we have also obtained access by faith into this grace in which we stand, and we rejoice in hope of the glory of God. More than that, we rejoice in our sufferings, knowing that suffering produces endurance, and endurance produces character, and character produces hope, and hope does not put us to shame, because God's love has been poured into our hearts through the Holy Spirit who has been given to us.

Mark 4:38-41 ESV / But he was in the stern, asleep on the cushion. And they woke him and said to him, "Teacher, do you not care that we are perishing?" And he awoke and rebuked the wind and said to the sea, "Peace! Be still!" And the wind ceased, and there was a great calm. He said to them, "Why are you so afraid? Have you still no faith?" And they were filled with great fear and said to one another, "Who then is this, that even the wind and the sea obey him?"

1 Timothy 6:12 ESV / Fight the good fight of the faith. Take hold of the eternal life to which you were called and about which you made the good confession in the presence of many witnesses.

Acts 14:22 ESV / Strengthening the souls of the disciples, encouraging them to continue in the faith, and saying that through many tribulations we must enter the kingdom of God.

Mark 11:22 ESV / And Jesus answered them, "Have faith in God.

Mark 5:36 ESV / But overhearing what they said, Jesus said to the ruler of the synagogue, "Do not fear, only believe."

Galatians 3:26 ESV / For in Christ Jesus you are all sons of God, through faith.

Romans 8:24-25 ESV / For in this hope we were saved. Now hope that is seen is not hope. For who hopes for what he sees? But if we hope for what we do not see, we wait for it with patience.

Romans 14:23 ESV / But whoever has doubts is condemned if he eats, because the eating is not from faith. For whatever does not proceed from faith is sin.

Proverbs 3:5 ESV / Trust in the Lord with all your heart, and do not lean on your own understanding.

Genesis 15:6 ESV / And he believed the Lord, and he counted it to him as righteousness.

James 2:26 ESV / For as the body apart from the spirit is dead, so also faith apart from works is dead.

Hebrews 10:38-39 ESV / But my righteous one shall live by faith, and if he shrinks back, my soul has no pleasure in him." But we are not of those who shrink back and are destroyed, but of those who have faith and preserve their souls

Galatians 2:20 ESV / I have been crucified with Christ. It is no longer I who live, but Christ who lives in me. And the life I now live in the flesh I live by faith in the Son of God, who loved me and gave himself for me.

Psalm 23:1-6 ESV / A Psalm of David. The Lord is my shepherd; I shall not want. He makes me lie down in green pastures. He leads me beside still waters. He restores my soul. He leads me in paths of righteousness for his name's sake. Even though I walk through the valley of the shadow of death, I will fear no evil, for you are with me; your rod and your staff, they comfort me. You prepare a table before me in the presence of my enemies; you anoint my head with oil; my cup overflows. ...

Luke 22:31-32 ESV / "Simon, Simon, behold, Satan demanded to have you, that he might sift you like wheat, but I have prayed for you that your faith may not fail. And when you have turned again, strengthen your brothers."

2 Timothy 1:7 ESV / For God gave us a spirit not of fear but of power and love and self-control.

Isaiah 41:10 ESV / Fear not, for I am with you; be not dismayed, for I am your God; I will strengthen you, I will help you, I will uphold you with my righteous right hand.

1 John 4:18 ESV / There is no fear in love, but perfect love casts out fear. For fear has to do with punishment, and whoever fears has not been perfected in love.

Psalm 34:4 ESV / I sought the Lord, and he answered me and delivered me from all my fears.

Proverbs 29:25 ESV / The fear of man lays a snare, but whoever trusts in the Lord is safe.

Philippians 4:6 ESV / Do not be anxious about anything, but in everything by prayer and supplication with thanksgiving let your requests be made known to God.

Romans 8:15 ESV / For you did not receive the spirit of slavery to fall back into fear, but you have received the Spirit of adoption as sons, by whom we cry, "Abba! Father!"

Psalm 56:3-4 ESV / When I am afraid, I put my trust in you. In God, whose word I praise, in God I trust; I shall not be afraid. What can flesh do to me?

Isaiah 43:1-3 ESV / But now thus says the Lord, he who created you, O Jacob, he who formed you, O Israel: "Fear not, for I have redeemed you; I have called you by name, you are mine. When you pass through the waters, I will be with you; and through the rivers, they shall not overwhelm you; when you walk through fire you shall not be burned, and the flame shall not consume you. For I am the Lord your God, the Holy One of Israel, your Savior. I give Egypt as your ransom, Cush and Seba in exchange for you.

Joshua 1:9 ESV / Have I not commanded you? Be strong and courageous. Do not be frightened, and do not be dismayed, for the Lord your God is with you wherever you go."

Psalm 27:1 ESV / Of David. The Lord is my light and my salvation; whom shall I fear? The Lord is the stronghold of my life; of whom shall I be afraid?

Psalm 125:1 ESV / A Song of Ascents. Those who trust in the Lord are like Mount Zion, which cannot be moved, but abides forever.

<u>1 Peter 2:17</u> ESV / Honor everyone. Love the brotherhood. Fear God. Honor the emperor.

<u>Deuteronomy 31:6</u> ESV / Be strong and courageous. Do not fear or be in dread of them, for it is the Lord your God who goes with you. He will not leave you or forsake you."

<u>Matthew 14:27</u> ESV / But immediately Jesus spoke to them, saying, "Take heart; it is I. Do not be afraid."

<u>Acts 27:24-25</u> ESV / And he said, 'Do not be afraid, Paul; you must stand before Caesar. And behold, God has granted you all those who sail with you.' So take heart, men, for I have faith in God that it will be exactly as I have been told.

<u>Isaiah 12:2</u> ESV / "Behold, God is my salvation; I will trust, and will not be afraid; for the Lord God is my strength and my song, and he has become my salvation."

Conduct Standards (Behavior in the Kingdom)

<u>1 Thessalonians 4:1-18</u> ESV / Finally, then, brothers, we ask and urge you in the Lord Jesus, that as you received from us how you ought to walk and to please God, just as you are doing, that you do so more and more. For you know what instructions we gave you through the Lord Jesus. For this is the will of God, your sanctification: that you abstain from sexual immorality; that each one of you know how to control his own body in holiness and honor, not in the passion of lust like the Gentiles who do not know God; ...

<u>Galatians 5:1-26</u> ESV / For freedom Christ has set us free; stand firm therefore, and do not submit again to a yoke of slavery. Look: I, Paul, say to you that if you accept circumcision, Christ will be of no advantage to you. I testify again to every man who accepts circumcision that he is obligated to keep the whole law. You are severed from Christ, you who would be justified by the law; you have fallen away from grace. For through the Spirit, by faith, we ourselves eagerly wait for the hope of righteousness. ...

<u>Galatians 2:20</u> ESV / I have been crucified with Christ. It is no longer I who live, but Christ who lives in me. And the life I now live in the flesh I live by faith in the Son of God, who loved me and gave himself for me.

<u>2 Corinthians 5:17</u> ESV / Therefore, if anyone is in Christ, he is a new creation. The old has passed away; behold, the new has come.

<u>1 Corinthians 10:31-33</u> ESV / So, whether you eat or drink, or whatever you do, do all to the glory of God. Give no offense to Jews or to Greeks or to the church of God, just as I try to please everyone in everything I do, not seeking my own advantage, but that of many, that they may be saved.

<u>1 Corinthians 6:9-10</u> ESV / Or do you not know that the unrighteous will not inherit the kingdom of God? Do not be deceived: neither the sexually immoral, nor idolaters, nor adulterers, nor men who practice homosexuality, nor thieves, nor the greedy, nor drunkards, nor revilers, nor swindlers will inherit the kingdom of God.

<u>Romans 13:1-7</u> ESV / Let every person be subject to the governing authorities. For there is no authority except from God, and those that exist have been instituted by God. Therefore whoever resists the authorities resists what God has appointed, and those who resist will incur judgment. For rulers are not a terror to good conduct, but to bad. Would you have no fear of the one who is in authority? Then do what is good, and you will receive his approval, for he is God's servant for your good. But if you do wrong, be afraid, for he does not bear the sword in vain. For he is the servant of God, an avenger who carries out God's wrath on the wrongdoer. Therefore one must be in subjection, not only to avoid God's wrath but also for the sake of conscience. ...

<u>Romans 8:1-39</u> ESV / There is therefore now no condemnation for those who are in Christ Jesus. For the law of the Spirit of life has set you free in Christ Jesus from the law of sin and death. For God has done what the law, weakened by the flesh, could not do. By sending his own Son in the likeness of sinful flesh and for sin, he condemned sin in the flesh, in order that the righteous requirement of the law might be fulfilled in us, who walk not according to the flesh but according to the Spirit. For those who live according to the flesh set their minds on the things of the flesh, but those who live according to the Spirit set their minds on the things of the Spirit. ...

<u>Luke 6:27-28</u> ESV / "But I say to you who hear, Love your enemies, do good to those who hate you, bless those who curse you, pray for those who abuse you."

<u>Psalm 37:8</u> ESV / Refrain from anger, and forsake wrath! Fret not yourself; it tends only to evil.

Proverbs 14:29 ESV / Whoever is slow to anger has great understanding, but he who has a hasty temper exalts folly.

Ephesians 4:26 ESV / Be angry and do not sin; do not let the sun go down on your anger,

James 1:19 ESV / Know this, my beloved brothers: let every person be quick to hear, slow to speak, slow to anger;

Ephesians 4:31 ESV / Let all bitterness and wrath and anger and clamor and slander be put away from you, along with all malice.

Proverbs 15:18 ESV / A hot-tempered man stirs up strife, but he who is slow to anger quiets contention.

Romans 12:19 ESV / Beloved, never avenge yourselves, but leave it to the wrath of God, for it is written, "Vengeance is mine, I will repay, says the Lord."

Proverbs 25:28 ESV / A man without self-control is like a city broken into and left without walls.

Philippians 2:14 ESV / Do all things without grumbling or questioning,

1 John 2:1-29 ESV / My little children, I am writing these things to you so that you may not sin. But if anyone does sin, we have an advocate with the Father, Jesus Christ the righteous. He is the propitiation for our sins, and not for ours only but also for the sins of the whole world. And by this we know that we have come to know him, if we keep his commandments. Whoever says "I know him" but does not keep his commandments is a liar, and the truth is not in him, but whoever keeps his word, in him truly the love of God is perfected. By this we may know that we are in him: ...

Psalm 37:7-9 ESV / Be still before the Lord and wait patiently for him; fret not yourself over the one who prospers in his way, over the man who carries out evil devices! Refrain from anger, and forsake wrath! Fret not yourself; it tends only to evil. For the evildoers shall be cut off, but those who wait for the Lord shall inherit the land.

Proverbs 6:34 ESV / For jealousy makes a man furious, and he will not spare when he takes revenge.

Matthew 6:33 ESV / 3 But seek first the kingdom of God and his righteousness, and all these things will be added to you.

Proverbs 28:27 ESV / Whoever gives to the poor will not want, but he who hides his eyes will get many a curse.

1 John 4:1 ESV / Beloved, do not believe every spirit, but test the spirits to see whether they are from God, for many false prophets have gone out into the world.

James 2:1-26 ESV / My brothers, show no partiality as you hold the faith in our Lord Jesus Christ, the Lord of glory. For if a man wearing a gold ring and fine clothing comes into your assembly, and a poor man in shabby clothing also comes in, and if you pay attention to the one who wears the fine clothing and say, "You sit here in a good place," while you say to the poor man, "You stand over there," or, "Sit down at my feet," have you not then made distinctions among yourselves and become judges with evil thoughts? Listen, my beloved brothers, has not God chosen those who are poor in the world to be rich in faith and heirs of the kingdom, which he has promised to those who love him? ...

Ephesians 4:14 ESV / So that we may no longer be children, tossed to and fro by the waves and carried about by every wind of doctrine, by human cunning, by craftiness in deceitful schemes.

1 Corinthians 10:24 ESV / Let no one seek his own good, but the good of his neighbor.

1 Corinthians 6:19 ESV / Or do you not know that your body is a temple of the Holy Spirit within you, whom you have from God? You are not your own,

Romans 16:17 ESV / I appeal to you, brothers, to watch out for those who cause divisions and create obstacles contrary to the doctrine that you have been taught; avoid them.

Romans 13:8-10 ESV / Owe no one anything, except to love each other, for the one who loves another has fulfilled the law. For the commandments, "You shall not commit adultery, You shall not murder, You shall not steal, You shall not covet," and any other commandment, are summed up in this word: "You shall love your neighbor as yourself." Love does no wrong to a neighbor; therefore love is the fulfilling of the law.

John 14:27 ESV / Peace I leave with you; my peace I give to you. Not as the world gives do I give to you. Let not your hearts be troubled, neither let them be afraid.

Matthew 7:1 ESV / "Judge not, that you be not judged"

Affirmative Action
(Favor)

Psalm 5:12 ESV / For you bless the righteous, O Lord; you cover him with favor as with a shield.

Psalm 90:17 ESV / Let the favor of the Lord our God be upon us, and establish the work of our hands upon us; yes, establish the work of our hands!

Psalm 102:13 ESV / You will arise and have pity on Zion; it is the time to favor her; the appointed time has come.

Ephesians 2:8-9 ESV / For by grace you have been saved through faith. And this is not your own doing; it is the gift of God, not a result of works, so that no one may boast.

Psalm 30:5 ESV / For his anger is but for a moment, and his favor is for a lifetime. Weeping may tarry for the night, but joy comes with the morning.

Genesis 39:4 ESV / So Joseph found favor in his sight and attended him, and he made him overseer of his house and put him in charge of all that he had.

Isaiah 58:11 ESV / And the Lord will guide you continually and satisfy your desire in scorched places and make your bones strong; and you shall be like a watered garden, like a spring of water, whose waters do not fail.

2 Corinthians 9:8-9 ESV / And God is able to make all grace abound to you, so that having all sufficiency in all things at all times, you may abound in every good work. As it is written, "He has distributed freely, he has given to the poor; his righteousness endures forever."

<u>Exodus 23:20</u> ESV / "Behold, I send an angel before you to guard you on the way and to bring you to the place that I have prepared.

Petition Procedure
(Prayer)

Philippians 4:6 ESV / Do not be anxious about anything, but in everything by prayer and supplication with thanksgiving let your requests be made known to God.

Mark 11:24 ESV / Therefore I tell you, whatever you ask in prayer, believe that you have received it, and it will be yours.

1 Thessalonians 5:17 ESV/ Pray without ceasing,

Matthew 6:7 ESV / "And when you pray, do not heap up empty phrases as the Gentiles do, for they think that they will be heard for their many words"

Luke 11:9 ESV / And I tell you, ask, and it will be given to you; seek, and you will find; knock, and it will be opened to you.

Romans 8:26 ESV / Likewise the Spirit helps us in our weakness. For we do not know what to pray for as we ought, but the Spirit himself intercedes for us with groanings too deep for words.

1 Timothy 2:1-4 ESV / First of all, then, I urge that supplications, prayers, intercessions, and thanksgivings be made for all people, for kings and all who are in high positions, that we may lead a peaceful and quiet life, godly and dignified in every way. This is good, and it is pleasing in the sight of God our Savior, who desires all people to be saved and to come to the knowledge of the truth.

Matthew 26:41 ESV / Watch and pray that you may not enter into temptation. The spirit indeed is willing, but the flesh is weak."

Jeremiah 33:3 ESV / Call to me and I will answer you, and will tell you great and hidden things that you have not known.

Compensation
(Sowing and Reaping)

Galatians 6:7 ESV / Do not be deceived: God is not mocked, for whatever one sows, that will he also reap.

2 Corinthians 9:6-8 ESV / The point is this: whoever sows sparingly will also reap sparingly, and whoever sows bountifully will also reap bountifully. Each one must give as he has decided in his heart, not reluctantly or under compulsion, for God loves a cheerful giver. And God is able to make all grace abound to you, so that having all sufficiency in all things at all times, you may abound in every good work.

Luke 6:38 ESV / "Give, and it will be given to you. Good measure, pressed down, shaken together, running over, will be put into your lap. For with the measure you use it will be measured back to you."

2 Corinthians 9:10-11 ESV / He who supplies seed to the sower and bread for food will supply and multiply your seed for sowing and increase the harvest of your righteousness. You will be enriched in every way to be generous in every way, which through us will produce thanksgiving to God.

1 Corinthians 13:3 ESV / If I give away all I have, and if I deliver up my body to be burned, but have not love, I gain nothing.

Galatians 6:6 ESV / One who is taught the word must share all good things with the one who teaches.

2 Corinthians 9:7 ESV / Each one must give as he has decided in his heart, not reluctantly or under compulsion, for God loves a cheerful giver.

Review

1. Therefore, we are a ________________ that lives in a ________________ that has a ________________.

2. God had to take His________________ and place it inside of us before we could become a living creature.

    a. Spirit

    b. Life

    c. Breath

    d. Soul

3. Our "Spirit" is the house in which we live in. (**TRUE or FALSE**)

4. He is God the ________________, the ________________, and the ________________.

5. The mind consists of the interconnecting parts, which are called the________________ and the________________.

6. The subconscious is the storehouse also known as the________________.

    a. Intellect

    b. Emotions

    c. Heart

    d. Memory

7. Our _____________ is dominated by the senses and also by what we think.

   a. Soul

   b. Body

   c. Imagination

   d. Emotions

8. As a man feels, so is he...   **(TRUE or FALSE)**

9. The way we think essentially will tell us how to feel... **(TRUE or FALSE)**

10. So God created man in His_____________.

11. We are ________________ beings having an __________________ experience on the earth.

12. God has a personal ________________ with mind and intelligence.

   a. Body

   b. Spirit

   c. Heart

   d. Relationship

13. Through ________________ we understand that the worlds were framed by the Word of God.

    a. Power

    b. Wisdom

    c. Insight

    d. Faith

14. Now hard work is the substance of things hoped for, the evidence of things not seen. (**TRUE or FALSE**)

15. God has dealt to every man the measure of faith. (**TRUE or FALSE**)

16. Whoever ________________ upon the Name of the Lord shall be ________________.

17. The Greek word for salvation is ________________________.

18. God so loved the ________________ that He ________________ His only begotten son.

19. We were originally created to have authority to rule in the earth. (**TRUE OR FALSE**)

20. We have a________________ world and a ________________ world.

21. The Kingdom of God is _________________ you.

22. God sent Jesus as a _________________ of the way we should live while living in the material world.

    a. Offering

    b. Example

    c. Inspiration

    d. Advocate

23. Bringing into captivity every _________________ to the obedience of Christ.

    a. Witness

    b. Devil

    c. Thought

    d. Heart

24. Grace is defined as "deserved" favor. **(TRUE or FALSE)**

25. Grace is the gift that came through obedience. **(TRUE or FALSE)**

26. In the Kingdom, we must live by

    _________________________________.

27. We must see the_________________________ of a thing in the spirit before we can see it materialize.

28. Faith is always _______.

    a. Power

    b. Wisdom

    c. Insight

    d. Now

29. Fear is designed to __________ progress.

    a. Promote

    b. Stimulate

    c. Increase

    d. Paralyze

30. Faith keeps you alive when everything around you appears to be dead. **(TRUE or FALSE)**

31. Faith is designed to produce things. **(TRUE or FALSE)**

32. The world system of buying and selling totally depends on the ___________________________.

33. ___________________ and _____________________ is a law in the Kingdom of God.

34. It is the responsibility of the President of the United States to take care of the poor. **(True or False)**

35. Not all are called to be _________ in the ministry.

36. It is important that we understand that we all have a ______________ in the kingdom.

37. What is an "Ambassador?"

   ____

38. What are the seven pillars (kingdoms) that operate in the world?

   ______________________   ______________________

   ______________________   ______________________

   ______________________   ______________________

          ____

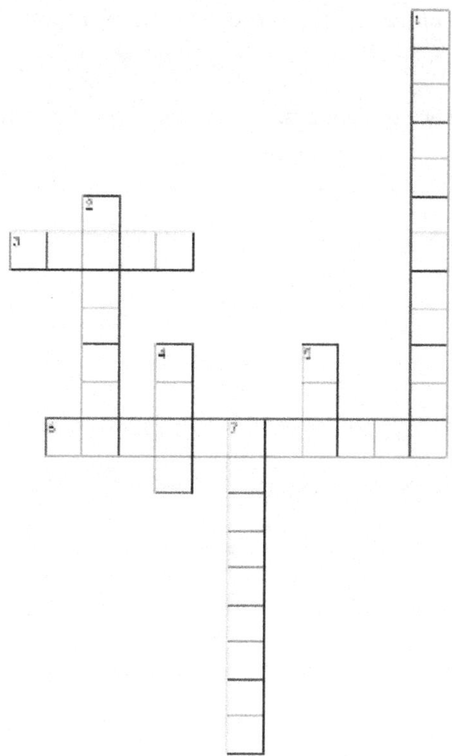

Across

3. 11:1 Now _______ is the substance of things hoped for, the evidence of things not seen

6. 2 Corinthians. 5:20 Now then we are _______________ for Christ

Down

1. 2 Corinthians. 10:5 Casting down _________________ and every high thing that exalts itself against the knowledge of Christ

2. Mt. 6:33 But seek first the __________ of God and His righteousness and all these things will be added unto you

4. 2 Tim. 1:7 God has not given us the spirit of ______, but of power and of love and a sound mind

5. Jn. 1:1 In the beginning was the Word, and the Word was with ____, and the Word was ____

7. Eph. 6:12 For we wrestle not against flesh and blood, but against...
____________ wickedness in high places

5. Jn. 1:1 In the beginning was the Word, and the Word was with ____, and the Word was ____

.

7. Eph. 6:12 For we wrestle not against flesh and blood, but against...
____________ wickedness in high places

I Am Daily Confessions –
Your Voice of Faith

I am made in the image of God, therefore,

I am a spirit that lives in a body that has a soul

I am an offspring of God

I am a kingdom citizen

I am an ambassador

I am a King in the earth

I am the head and not the tail above only and not beneath

I am blessed

I am more than a conqueror

I am operating by faith

I am Favored

I am healed

I am saved

I am the righteousness of God

I am a branch of the true vine

I am redeemed

I am justified

I am a friend of God

I am free from the law of sin and death

I am a fellow heir with Christ

I am blessed with every spiritual blessing in heavenly places

I am chosen Holy and blameless before the Lord

I now live under the Grace of God

I am God's workmanship created to produce good works

I am a member of Christ's body and a partaker of His promises
I am loved by God
I am in purpose and I am operating in purpose daily
I am always in the right place at the right time with the right
understanding
I am led by the spirit of God I do not follow the voice of a stranger
I am ONLY what God says that I am

Daily Faith Confession

I am the righteousness of God; therefore, I live by faith. There isn't anything that is impossible for me because I can do ALL things through Christ who gives me strength. I am filled with the knowledge of wisdom therefore; I am never caught off guard. When I open my mouth, God fills it. Fear does not live in me, and God has rescued me from every trap. My faith leads me, shields me, and my confidence in Christ has healed me. I am covered by the blood of the lamb from the crown of my head to the bottom of my feet; therefore, I clearly understand that with the greater one in me I shall not face defeat. There isn't anything that I will be faced with today that God has not already delivered me from. I walk in assurance of the WORD of God without wavering. All of His answers to me are yes and AMEN! By faith, I will accomplish everything that YOU would have me do on today without any distractions, hindrances, setbacks or set ups from the adversary. I have confessed this with my mouth, I believe it in my heart, and therefore, I consider it DONE, in JESUS' NAME, Amen!

Scriptures

Romans 8:30

Hebrews 10:38

Philippians 4: 13

Colossians 1:19

Palms 81:10

2 Timothy 1:7

Palms 91

Psalms 107:2

2 Corinthians 1:20

Isaiah 53:5

1 Peter 2:24

For more information about Dr. Williams please email her at <u>fromtheinsideout2015@gmail.com</u>